For You From Sascha

Old and new thoughts of comfort

and understanding for healing from grief

by
Alexandra Sascha Wagner

Writers Club Press
San Jose · New York · Lincoln · Shanghai

For You From Sascha
Copyright © 1999 Alexandra Sascha Wagner

This book may not be reproduced or distributed, in whole or in part, in print or by any other means without the written permission of the author.

You can contact Alexandra Sascha Wagner at:
Sascha10@aol.com.

ISBN: 1-893652-18-1

Library of Congress Catalog Card Number: 99-62743

This book was published using the on-line/on-demand publishing services of Writers Club Press, an imprint of iUniverse, Inc.

For information address:
iUniverse.com, Inc.
620 North 48th Street
Suite 201
Lincoln, NE 68504-3467
www.iUniverse.com

URL: http://www.writersclub.com

This collection of thoughts for grievers and their friends is dedicated with greatest affection to
In Loving Memory
the Fourth National Conference for parents without
surviving children, convened in Vienna, Virginia on May 27, 1999

Contents

Introduction		1
I.	Early Grief	3
II.	Help and Solace	21
III.	Memories	57
IV.	Days and Seasons	79
V.	The Road Ahead	125

The author thanks:

Shirley Bryant and Nyssa

Diana Woodson

Donnafred Hinman

Sharon Marshall

Sally Migliaccio

Kim Stoddard Gerringer

Genesse Gentry

for their invaluable help in selecting and correcting texts for these pages.

INTRODUCTION

These pages are intended to give the reader a few moments of comfort in the journey from grief to hope and new beginnings. We realize that grievers are not always willing or able to concentrate on long chapters and learned text. Therefore, this little volume presents its writings in briefest form, one page or two at a time.

With few exceptions, text on these pages has been reprinted in newsletters and commercial publications — and if this small collection makes grieving time even a little bit easier, it serves its purpose.

Whether your grief is new or not: when it seems that no one quite understands you or when you want to share grief feelings, these pages try to help you find consolation, comfort and courage.

Once more, I am grateful for having been invited into a place close to your heart.

Sascha

(FROM ONE WHO KNOWS)

I promise you, my friend.
I promise you
that you will feel
the warmth of spring again,
that you will touch
the hands of children
and the lips of lovers
and the tenderness of Christmas again.

But here and now, my friend,
I promise consolation:
Some morning you will see
beauty in your sorrow,
comfort in the wealth of love remembered,
courage in the aching tide of days.

I promise you, my friend. I promise you
that you will understand
some day
some day
this pain which taught you
what depth and height
and greatness
and devotion
one life can hold.
YOUR life, my friend.

I. EARLY GRIEF

For You From Sascha

EARLY GRIEF

I feel a lightless void inside.
It has no name.
I know that others say
I am in grief.
But for me,
it is without a name,
a mortal distress
beyond words.

Early Grief

WORDS

When grief is new
you need not find a reason
however good and brave
to temper your despair.

When grief is new
the heart accepts no answer
however wise and kind
to ease your mourning.

When grief is new
your life can only know
disintegration,
overwhelming pain...

> My friend, try to believe
> what other grievers learned:
> you will not always hurt
> as you hurt now;
> time will restore
> the soundness of your mind.

(All other words
are shadows on the wind
when grief is new).

For You From Sascha

ICE AGE

Yesterday you were with me
like a cool day in summer,
like a radiant song,
buoying my spirit.

Today you are gone,
and it is as if an ice age
has taken my life away.

Early Grief

PROCESS

I am standing aside,
seeing myself
with my own eyes,
but uninvolved.
I observe myself
in the process of losing myself.

Previously published in Eva Lager's book,
" Knowing Why Changes Nothing"

For You From Sascha

LIMBO

What is the use of living?
What is the use of my life?
I struggle for its healing,
but is it worth the struggle?

I have heard
so many proclamations
about life and its noble design.
But I am no longer convinced.
My life seems worthless.
Living itself seems worthless.

What am I healing
when I heal myself?

previously published in Eva Lager's book,
" Knowing Why Changes Nothing"

Early Grief

CONFUSION

Confusion of the mind –
always the question: Why?
Not even certain
what the question means.

What do I want to know?
Why do I want to know
when knowing changes nothing.

And more than ever
haunts me that savage
inquisition of despair:
Why do I live?
Why do I have to live?
Why do I have to live now?

previously published in Eva Lager's book,
"In Knowing Why Changes Nothing"

For You From Sascha

A LIFE LOST

I have lost a life
    - not my own.
But it would have been easier
to have lost my own life
than to have lost
the life I loved more than my own.

Early Grief

THEY SPEAK OF HOPE

Hope for a better future?
    What is a better future
    when you have had to lose
    that life so close to you?

    Hope for feeling better?
        What does feeling better mean
        when grief has mutilated
        all feeling?

Hope for hurting less?
    How can you hurt less
    when you are in an anguish
    beyond pain?

Only you have the answer.
    Find out what hope means
                for you.

For You From Sascha

WANTING

Walking out of long
and aching night,
wanting to be child and at home,
    wanting to feel warm.

Walking into a strange
and distant day ...
wanting to weep and to sing,
    wanting to feel safe.

Walking along a dark
and haunted road,
wanting to find and be found,
    wanting to feel peace.

Early Grief

CHANGES

Be aware that new grief
changes all of your emotions
for a time.

But grief does not change
all of your emotions
forever!

Some of your old feelings
will return to you.
Be patient.
Please be patient.

For You From Sascha

INCIDENT BEFORE DAWN

You walk through the house
looking for something...
Your keys?
Your glasses?
No, weren't you looking
for that old address book?

    You walk through the house,
    feeling like something lost...
    Are you looking for yourself?
        You walk through the house...
        Are you losing your mind?
        How can you tell?

You walk through the house
looking for something.
Are you trying not to remember
what you have lost?

    (You will find your glasses
        or your keys
        or your old address book
        or yourself and your mind
        in the morning.
                        But ...)

Early Grief

THOUGHTS FOR SPRINGTIME?

Would it be easier,
    if spring were not so lovely?

Would it be easier,
    if robins did not sing?

Would I be stronger,
    if the trees were barren
    or if a cloak of gray
        hid everything?

Could I be braver,
    if the days were faded
    and if the sun remained
        remote and cold?

I hear the whispers
of a new beginning.
    The earth is new.
    Why is my grief so old?

For You From Sascha

In your gathering

of memories,

invite your courage

to remember

everything.

Early Grief

SOLACE

In the smallest hour of your day,
when you are alone
with things remembered,
questions unanswered
and unfinished dreams,
    then:

    give to yourself
        the gifts of your kindness,
    bring to yourself
        the comforts of forgiveness,
    share with yourself
        the mercy of your love.

For You From Sascha

HOLD ME

I want to cry.
Just sometime, let me cry.
Do not demand
that constant smile from me.

I know you are
uneasy with my tears.
I need to cry.
Please, do not turn away.

I promise you
that I will smile again.
Tomorrow I will be as light as air.

But hold me now
and let my sorrow be.
Just for today,
this moment: let me cry.

Early Grief

FIRST ENCOUNTER

When grief first enters our life,
it tends to invade us —
completely and relentlessly.
We are without comfort, we do not feel pleasure,
we find no joy.
We ache in mind and body.
We feel weak and numb.
In the deepest core of our being,
we are ready to accept
that we will never know happiness again.
What's more, we feel that this state
is entirely appropriate, natural and irreversible.
Nothing can convince us that,
given time,
we can learn to live again.

But we will.

NEW GRIEF

The first weeks and months after bereavement can be terrifying. It seems as if the pain stays at a monotonous peak; it seems as if one's mind will be lost at any moment. And although most of us "get better" after the first terror, we usually do not realize that until we look back years later.

When we think about it, this state of affairs is almost "reasonable". After such an overwhelmingly traumatic experience, we can fall – as it were – to the end of the world. Coming back from there is bound to be slow beyond our imagination and fraught with reversals. So far, no one has found a method to avoid this painful journey back. Perhaps it will help to hear that you have already begun to travel. You will find it is a long journey, and desperately hard – and you may often almost want to stay where you are. But you will realize, later, that the wind of tomorrow is even now stretching your sails, and life waits for you across the sea.

If you only knew...

II. HELP AND SOLACE

For You From Sascha

Grief is the ceremony
of lost treasure.
Grief is the homage
you pay to the love
you were once blessed to share.
Grief is not an enemy.

Help And Solace

SMALL HAND

The small hand
that held your hand -
how long ago -

The small hand
now holds your heart
against bitterness.

The small hand
that held your hand
can heal your life.

For You From Sascha

IT IS TRUE

"You will not always hurt like this".
These words are true.

If they do not reach
your heart today,
do not reject them:
keep them in your mind.

    One morning –
not tomorrow perhaps,
but the day after tomorrow,
or the month after next month.

    One morning the dawn will wake you
    with the inconceivable surprise:
Your grief will have lost
one small moment of its force.

Be ready for the time
when you can feel for yourself
that these words are true:
    "You will not always hurt like this".

Help And Solace

ENDOWMENT

Hope gives us vision for regaining
the tenderness of memories.
Hope carries us through
to survival and healing.

Hope offers us courage
for acceptance and overcoming.
Hope gives us
new spirit and new laughter.

Hope is among the greatest gifts
to be found in time of sorrow.
But hope cannot restore
what is lost to death.
Hope can only go forward
and make us new.

Give space to hope in your life.

For You From Sascha

POSITIVES ON HOLD

You may not want to accept yet that some of your old feelings, your former self, will ever return to you. Or that some new feelings of hope and courage will come - often unexpectedly - into your shaken life. Even if you do not think you want to leave a 'mental door' open for your future, reinvested, you may try accepting an awareness of positive things.

After your unmitigated sorrow begins to soften, you could find it possible to take mental notes when you observe that something nice has happened, although you should not expect to find such an event 'enjoyable.'

At first, you will most likely be unable to smile at anything. Just register briefly whatever small positives catch your attention. You might say something like 'this would be pleasant, if I felt better.' As always, remind yourself not to rush. When you are ready to recognize positives, however, you will benefit from guiding yourself gently to acknowledge these, one very small step at a time.

You know how seriously grief has damaged your ability to see beyond the dark side of existence.

In noting positives whenever you can, you improve your chance at healing and your readiness for your happier memories.

Help And Solace

UNEASY WORD

Hope is not an easy word for grievers –
    but we, more than most others,
    need to understand
      what hope can mean for us.

Hope means finding the strength
    to live with grief.
Hope means nurturing with grace
    the joy of remembrance.
Hope means embracing
    with tenderness and pride
    our own life
    and the gifts left to us
    by those we have lost.

For You From Sascha

HEALING TAKES TIME

Did you wake up in the morning
with tears in your heart?
And did you say to yourself
"I should not feel like crying,
not like this, every morning."?

But you do know the truth, don't you?
When life deals us such a tragic blow,
such enormous damage,
we need many mornings to recover.
We need more than a few moments
            to heal.

Take for yourself the grace
of one quiet healing-step at a time.
Trying to rush the work of grief
will slow down your renewal.

You only need to recognize
that you WILL recover some day.
You only need to remember
that we all have our own measure,
and we all heal at our own pace.

Help And Solace

NEAR DEATH

There are many ways
in which to have near-death experiences.
Being near-death can mean
being too close to death,
as you were
when your child died.

When grief
almost takes your own life away,
remind yourself that,
not long ago,
you were too close to death,
and now you need time
to heal from that encounter.

Say to yourself
"I will begin to heal
when my life recovers."
"I will begin to heal
when a smile can again
touch my heart."
"I will begin to heal
when I can."

For You From Sascha

IN THE MORNING

From wherever you are
    you smile at me.
"Find life for both of us,"
    you say.
"Find peace for both of us,"
    you say.
"Find strength and love and hope
    for both of us,
      because you are
        my mother."

Help And Solace

THE PRICE

It is not a question
of whether I could have wanted
never to have you with me,
if had I known
how deeply your dying
would break my life today.

There is only one certain truth:
Even if I had known
that there would come to me
the cruel grief I suffer today,
I would endure it all again
for the wonder of
having had you in my life.

For You From Sascha

ANSWERS?

The memories are
bright and far away,
because
in all those grieving years
the pain has calmed.
The mind has learned
that life and loss are brothers,
that Death tells nothing,
when we ask him 'why'.

The memories are
deep and long ago.
Here,
after all those grieving years,
the songs we sang,
the thoughts we shared,
the morning kisses,
and the mystic evenings,
remain alive in us
and unforgotten.

Now Love holds answers,
though we ask her nothing.

Help And Solace

WINDOWS

The breath of winter
painted fragile stars
on all the windows
of my quiet house.

And there I found
your face,
more fragile even
than the season's art,
a wonder to my eyes.

How can it be
that winter paints
such secret things
in white-and-silver sheen
for those who cry alone
at frosted windows?

For You From Sascha

WHAT WILL YOU FIND?

In everyone,
there is a secret place,
where the sorrow
    of a lifetime
tries to hide
from the painful touch
of recognition –
Good friend,
    if you share
    your secret place
    what will you find?

Help And Solace

SUNSHINE THOUGHT

Deep in winter, my friend,
when life is darkest,
it is very important
to try thinking
one small sunshine thought
every morning, early.
Try your best.

For You From Sascha

CAN YOU REMEMBER?

With winter tumbling snow
— the roses silent
and the water ice ...

    with trees so barren
    that your mind refuses
    to picture leaves
    and green and even blossoms

        can you remember,
        can you feel again,
        that spring did come
        from winter, every year?

Help And Solace

FRIENDS

When our special sadness
comes to call,
when we remember
more than we can bear,
when courage falters –
shadows everywhere,
then let us reach
and touch and share,
we, who are friends.

For You From Sascha

EMISSARIES

My flowers lie with impersonal faces
on the ground where she rests.
My flowers do not speak,
they do not sing.
They only move
as the wind may touch them
or my hands.
But these flowers hide within them
the tenderness and the sorrow
of my grieving –
That is their secret, and mine.

    Knowing Why Changes Nothing
        By Eva Lager

MESSAGE

When the child you have cherished is taken,
when the light of that promise is gone,
when the faith which sustained you, is shaken
and your days stumble painfully on,

When the sorrows of loss are unending
and your God seems forever away,
find the message your lost-one keeps sending:
words of loving and thanking and mending...
let your child shape the peace of your day.

For You From Sascha

THE ONLY CHILD

Words are so small.
Words are too commonplace.
How do I speak
the meaning of that face?

Face of my child,
face of my child who died,
light of my world,
stay shining at my side.

Help And Solace

ISLANDS

Look for
the small,
quiet islands of peace
that arise
unexpectedly
from out of
the great sea
of your sorrow.

For You From Sascha

LOSSES AND GAINS

In time of grieving,
you may encounter
      other unexpected losses...

Friends you counted on
may not be able
to stand with you,
may not be able
to give themselves to your need.

      But you will also find
      some unexpected gains:
      people you never counted on
      will be your friends
      and stand with you
      and give you strength.

They are the treasures
you will learn to cherish,
when you begin to heal.

Help And Solace

ABOUT BEING STRONG

Many people are convinced
that being strong and brave
means trying to think
and talk about "something else."

But we know
that being strong and brave
means thinking and talking
about your dead love,
until your grief begins to be bearable.

That is strength.
That is courage.
And only thus can
"being strong and brave"
help you to heal.

For You From Sascha

MASKS

At times of sorrow
everyone deals with feeling
in unique ways.

Try not to be hurt
if those closest to your heart
seem to grieve less
or behave strangely.

We cannot always see on the outside
how someone mourns on the inside.

Help And Solace

LIFELINK

Find in the dark of grief
the sunlit spaces.
Find in your sorrowed time
a moment's smile.
Find in the loneliness
of your despairing
one warm and kindred mind,
one hand to touch
your most secluded feeling.

           -Find a friend.

For You From Sascha

WHO IS TO SAY ——

Love and death
are the most powerful events
in human experience.

Joy and grief
are the natural companions
of love and death.

>Who is to say
>that we could have
>love and joy
>if we had not
>death and grief?

Help And Solace

SHARING

When the most fearful solitude
    seems yours alone,
    when you are certain
    that there are no friends,
that no one feels as cast away as you –
when night and day and earth
    move on without you
and leave you, motionless, in icy pain –

when you feel mute with grief and isolation,
    when you seem cut
    from every living thing,
then listen to the truth
    your silence touches:

Behind oblique facades
    of noise and cheering
a thousand other lives
    are drowning, drowning,
in other sorrows and in other pain –
    afraid to cry for help,
afraid to break....

They need to hear your sorrow
    and your darkness.
Give them your truest self,
    discover theirs.
Reveal your tears –
    then share and speak your heart

For You From Sascha

MIDNIGHT GIFTS

The grief
that takes
your sleep away
at midnight,
it brings you hurt.
It also brings you love.

Help And Solace

HONESTY

There is an honesty
to comfort us –
an honesty
that does not shrink
from sorrow –
an honesty
that lets us recognize
how life is more
than ignorance of pain.

There is an honesty
to give us hope-
an honesty
that sings the song of life
and keeps us singing
even while we grieve.

There is an honesty
to let us reach
for all of life's horizons,
as far as the heart can see.

For You From Sascha

ANGER

Grief often brings to us
a feeling of desperate anger.

But let us try to remember
that much of our anger is only
a reflection of helplessness
in the face of death.

Yet, that anger must be acknowledged —
anger denied
is an enemy of healing.

Help And Solace

FACETS

Grief casts a sharper edge on every day
and deepens all the shadows in your life.
    For you, whose grief is not
    one grief alone,
    those shadows have
    the sharpest edge of all,
        because the grief
        besieging you tonight
        restores again
        too many other sorrows
        and disappointments raging in your heart.

Grief asks so many questions, answers few —
grief takes away your patience and your peace.
    For you, whose grief means
    losing everything,
    those questions have
    the sharpest edge of all.

There is but half an answer
weeping in the silence:
Find comfort and endure.
Remember love.
        And wait.

For You From Sascha

DARK DAY

On a very dark day in winter;
    when your eyes have forgotten
    the color of apple trees...
    On a very dark day in winter,
    count the days until spring.

    On a very dark day in winter
    when your mind can't remember
    the color of memories ...
    On a very dark day in winter,
    reach for the healing kindness
        of time.

Help And Solace

SOUNDINGS

The world may wonder:
    are we bound by death,
    we who have lost the child
    whose breath we shared.

The world should know:
    though we may cry at night,
    we are not strangers
    to the art of laughter.

And sometimes
    we reach deeper into life.
    Has death then left us
    with a finer ear
    for listening to the song
    of other children?

For You From Sascha

COUNSELOR

Find for yourself
the same kindness
as you would feel
for your very best friend.
> What would you say to her,
> if she were lost
> in guilty doubt
> as you are now?

Would you not
counsel compassion
instead of finding fault
or giving useless advice?
Would you not
counsel tenderness
and soothing comfort
for her anguished spirit?

Listen to yourself.
you can be
your own best counselor.

Help And Solace

SOBBING OUT LOUD

Do you wonder
if we should encourage each other to sob out loud?
Even sobbing out loud alone is better
than not sobbing at all.
    Some human cultures
    provide grievers with rituals
    for sobbing and screaming,
    like the women in some African villages,
    or the bereaved mothers of Islam,
    whom we should envy
    for the tradition
    of giving sound to their grief.
        And what about grieving men?
        Have we become so "civilized"
        that we can only weep quietly?
            Perhaps we should all learn
            not to sob
            in silence.

FOR DONNAFRED

Behind

each dark flower of sorrow

waits a memory

of the blessings

you shared.

III. MEMORIES

For You From Sascha

THE OTHER SEASON

Look to the season of your memories –
it fills the weather of your life
    with mildness.
It turns to laughter what your love
    remembers:
the sound of words, invented new
    for singing,
discovery of all-important secrets.

Look to the season of your memories –
how rich you were, and be how rich again.
Look to the season of your memories:
mourn and recall the child you love,
    you love……
until you lose yourself
    to find yourself.

Memories

WARM WINTER DAY

How welcome
right now, right here –
at the beginning of one more year –
 is this day
with a kindness like summer.

Memories
shine in the sun:
right here, right now,
out of the gray
we call winter
 warms you
the thought of a child.

For You From Sascha

HEARTFROST

Does it not seem
as if in wintertime
your mind remembers
all those sunny things
that warmed you once?
And does it seem
as if you have not smiled
forever?

Now take your hands,
one in the other hand,
and do remember
all those sunny things
again.
Again.
And let them warm you now.
— The smile will find you.

Memories

FOUR A.M.

And does the bitter grief
keep you awake?
    Look at it full,
    as you would look
    into an avalanche
    sweeping your life away.

        Look at that bitter grief
        with conscious eyes,
        as you have looked on death.
        And tell your brooding sorrow:
        Yes, you know that death demands
        unwavering attention.

Do not avoid the truth
your mind repeats, repeats ...

        And then there comes a truth
        beyond the truth –
        (no, do not turn away).
            Into your bitterness,
            love finds a way
            to give you solace.

        And, yes, your heart will know
        the sun when night has ended.

For You From Sascha

ORACLE

Your child has died
      and only this is certain:
      that you will never be
      the same again-
      not what you were-
      not what you might have been.
Your child has died
      and grief may touch your vision
      with new and restless lights,
      with want and pain
      where once your life
      found reason strength and peace.
Your child has died.
      The face of god is changing.
      It may be closer
      and more careful now
      or may seem cold
      and cruel far away.
So trust your soul
      (however bright or somber
      however calm or fierce).
      Trust in your soul:
      — it will declare
            your answer and your hope.

      In time ………………….

Memories

When your grief
    is without memories,
    let your heart find
    the memories
    that might have been.

For You From Sascha

LESSON?

Grief shows you who are
more even than love,
or success, or adventure.
More than any other experience,
grief shows you who you are.

    When a few moments of calm
    begin to find you,
    remember what grief has taught you
    and who you are.

Memories

JOURNEY

Life is a journey
between shadow and light
many times over.

Travel your road
with readiness, always, for joy
and with loving attention
to the richness
      of your memories.

For You From Sascha

LEAVING

Saying good-bye
    is not an easy departure.

Saying good-bye
    is not a breath and a smile.

Saying good-bye
    makes us feel frail and uncertain.

Saying good-bye
    takes one's composure away.

Saying good-bye
    even if only to travel,
    even if not for an "always"
    even if just changing place....

Saying good-bye
    means a mysterious future.

Saying good-bye
    conjures reminders of loss.

Thank you again
    for all the love and the sharing.

Tell me good-bye
    that I may travel in peace.

Memories

MODEST TRIUMPH

Death has been in my house
too many times.
Death ran against my life
with poison lance.
Death took away tomorrow
in a shroud ...

      But death forgot to claim
      my love for beauty,
      ears for those summers past,
      eyes for the fragrant snow
      of bygone winters...

      And death left to my mind
      the recollections
      of unspoken music...

      Yes, death left to my mind
      those many tears
      those many smiles
      to keep me whole.

For You From Sascha

SONG

A song is on my mind -
a pleasant song, simple
and almost lighthearted.

Nothing else on my mind,
only the song,
singing itself over and over
all day long.

It is not a song about you,
but it is a song because of you.
And it means
that I miss you
all day long.

Memories

VESPERS

Just at sunset
does your busy day
suddenly fall silent
and remember?

Does the rising night
make you ready
to see that face again,
to feel that love?

Let the sunset
weave its magic.
Invite the rising night
to cast its dream.

Have we not said
a thousand times and more
that we are richest
when the heart remembers?

For You From Sascha

HUSBAND

I saw the grief
behind your earnest eyes.
(You would give anything
to have your child again.)

I felt the helplessness
behind your silent anguish.
(You would give anything
to take this hurt away.)

    I know you learned
    to keep your tears in hiding.
    And you were taught
    few words to speak for solace.
    not yours, not mine.

I saw the grief
behind your earnest eyes.
And I will know
to understand and trust you,
loving father.

Memories

SIDE EFFECTS

Bereavement often has unanticipated side effects. Why do some friends desert us when we grieve? One explanation may be that a griever's friend has a LOT of extra obligations.

Grievers are not the easiest company. They often are a heavy mixture of guilt, anger, pain, love and confusion. That is difficult or uncomfortable for many people to handle.

— And all too often the griever is unable to deal with such a failing and feels deeply hurt. -

We can probably agree that it SHOULD be the helper's task to bear with the momentary hardship....... But many times, grief becomes a time of mutual disappointment.

When the most painful time of your grieving starts to fade, look at such disappointments and decide whether you ought to forgive AND forget. We all have our limitations.............

For You From Sascha

RELEVANT QUESTION

Sooner or later you will ask yourself
whether your anger is greater
than your determination to survive.

Does your anger keep you
from loving those near and dear to your heart?
Do you think your anger should be
the same five years from now?

In many ways you may recognize
that love and peace of mind
are more important
than most mistakes.
Think about it?

Memories

The past is part of us

and our future.

He who tells us to forget

does not understand

the past

    or

        the future.

For You From Sascha

EXERCISE (for Next Week?)

Try to teach yourself to remember
at the end of each day
that something nice
or important
or funny
or interesting
or beautiful
has happened to you ...

Even though you may not be able
to enjoy such things just then,
keep your mind aware.

Memories

IMAGE

A breath of summertime
drifts from the rising sun,
comes from beyond the trees,
hums at your window –

A breath of summertime
smiles at your dusty face,
weaves into cloud and light
visions remembered –

A breath of summertime
touches your secret tears,
brushes the tears away –
(but not the image)

For You From Sascha

CANDLES

It is not easy to remember dead children.

But, easy or not,
we know that we will not —
and do not want to —
forget them.

Therefore we reach out together again,
to love them and to celebrate their memory.

Again, we light their special candles
and we say their beloved names.

We remember our children, who died.
They remain forever part of us,
and we are richer for having shared their lives,
 however briefly.

Memories

LEGACY

Memories are a legacy
of hope and courage,
left to help us go on
when the giver is gone.

AT DUSK

Light a quiet candle.
Blow a quiet kiss.
Say a quiet fare-thee-well
to the one you miss.

Light a quiet candle.
Shed a quiet tear.
Sing a quiet lullaby
and the quiet Christmas Star
      will hear.

IV. DAYS AND SEASONS

For You From Sascha

YOU ARE CALLED

Into the rivers of eternity
The human mind adds, new,
a grain of time
and calls it by its weighty name:
One year.

Friend, you are called
to be a part of it,
part of this year-
and part, however small,
of universe and of eternity.

Days And Seasons

ANOTHER YEAR

Old year has gone away
with gift and candle –
old year has gone away
with thought and song.

Old year has given light
and dark and season.
Old year has been too short
and been too long.

>Old year has given joy
>and disappointment.
>Old year has given grief
>and strength to cope.
>Old year was memory
>and was forgetting –
>>Another year is come.
>>Give it your hope.

For You From Sascha

FULL CIRCLE

The year has gone again
from spring to winter -
and in this year;
your memories may have found
a breath of calm between them,
quiet respite - sometimes.

Then why must there be
twice as many now -
these feelings, now,
these visions, songs and voices,
from Halloween to New Year's:
Twice memories and smiles
Twice memories and tears...

You know the answer,
even while you cry:
your tears are
(like your smiles)
the season's face of love.

Days And Seasons

VALENTINE'S DAY

Did you know?

When we truly listen

    to each other,

  we are saying

      ~~ I love you ~~

For You From Sascha

ABOUT FEELING GUILTY

Do you blame yourself?
Are you strangled by the burden
of things you think you "should have done,"
as if these were the things
that killed him?

Dear Griever,
take time to realize
that death is not in your hands,
and blame is not the answer.

Try to relinquish
this relentless torment.
Hold your heart now
with the tenderness
that human grief deserves.

Days And Seasons

IN MARCH

The year moves on.
Between the weeks and days
are spaces filled
with more than only time:
those minutes, moments,
when your life stands still
and aches in memory...

And part of you
needs to endure the dark,
because it means
to have that love again.
And part of you
prays for forgetfulness,
because your mind
may break, remembering.

Between the weeks and days
are spaces filled
with more than only time.

For You From Sascha

SPRING, SOON

Is this our season
more than some other
turn of the year?
Is it?

With winter dancing
out and in,
freezing the melted snow
one more time?

Is this the season
between death and life.
Is it?

With sorrow struggling
in and out,
finding the touch of hope
one more time?

Days And Seasons

PASSOVER

Counting the years,
Blessings and tears,
Counting the children
Who are gone
      From this earth.

Counting the memories
Of times past and done.
Blessing the children
On earth in this day of life.

For You From Sascha

APRIL

Time for jesting?
Time for laughter?

And if you are not ready,
not yet,
to remember something
that makes you laugh,

Tell April to be patient.
Take your time.

THE CHILDREN OF APRIL NINETEENTH

    Let these children
    forever remind us
    that our souls may be
    in greater peril than theirs.
    Let these children
    forever remind us
    that we are the ones
    to need their blessings now.
    Let these children
    remind us to pray
    that time has not run out
        for us.

In memory of the children who died in Oklahoma City and of all children in the world who fall victim to the mindless cruelties of our time.

For You From Sascha

SPRING/TIME

The days are getting longer, longer,
and it is easier to work away.
So many things to do…. keep busy, busy.
The more we do, the less we have to say.

The days are getting warmer, softer –
and is it easier to work a lot?
Alright, forgive yourself for crying midnights;
the heart remembers what your hands forgot!

MOTHER'S DAY

How is the weather now,
on mother's day?
Shining with spring,
promising early roses?

But hides there, in secret,
a moment of grief?
Frost in the sunlight,
pale heartache of sorrow?

The children are gone. –
Are you reminded twice over:
the children are gone?

And will you be ready perhaps
to remember without tears
the sunlight, the laughter, the roses,
you shared with the children
on next mother's day?

For You From Sascha

JUST SPRING?

This is no ordinary spring at all.
It dances on with unbecoming weather:
now more like winter than December was,
and then again as soft as early summer.

This is no ordinary spring at all.
It meets your heart with
          unexpected dangers:
now with the loneliest of memories,
and then again with unforgotten laughter.

This is no ordinary spring at all.
This is like life itself, a changing season.
Accept the wintertime of grief and then
reach for the hope of summer and of healing.

Days And Seasons

MAY MORNING

The morning colors
love and ache together
into the shape that life intends to be:
—As memories whelm secret territories,
    your mind takes note
       of sorrow, time and place.

The morning moves you
through familiar paces.
—While thought confirms another day in spring,
    your heart reminds you
       that your child is gone.

For You From Sascha

LILACS

Come, look at May with me.
The world is music.
The lilacs laugh
and every meadow sings.

Your heart forgets to think
of spring or summer,
forgets the grief
that happened in the snow,

until a memory
moves into sunlight
to bring the child,
the child who is not here.

Still, look at May with me
and find the music.
And - for a moment -
hear the lilacs weep.

Days And Seasons

MEMORIAL DAY

For each grave
Where a soldier lies
At his rest

For each prayer
That is said today
Out of love

For each sigh
Of remembering
Someone who died

Let us also give thought to
The mothers and fathers
The brothers and sisters
The friends and the lovers
Whom death left behind.

For You From Sascha

SCHOOL'S OUT

That time of year again,
when children move
from classroom to reality.

And deeper even than before
your heart recalls the child
who left this life
to move from here
to ultimate reality.

Give blessing to that journey,
when you can.

Days And Seasons

FATHERS DAY

Warm and sunny day in June,
father's day.
Children, small and grown
give gifts to father
say thanks to father
say I love you.

But there are fathers
whose children are not here
to give gifts and say thanks
and say I love you.

Remember the fathers
whose children are gone,
because all too often
they grieve in heartbreak silence.

For You From Sascha

AUGUST

The summer runs to harvest –
Do you ask:
How can a harvest be without my child?

    Friend, some day soon
    the harvest in your life
    will bring you hope and wealth
        from love remembered.

Days And Seasons

VACATION

I still remember
when I could not sleep
at three a.m.
Awake and dark,
I did not want forgetting
night after night.
                Night after night.

I still remember
when I could not sleep
at three a.m.
Alone and mute
I sobbed the same old questions
into my mind.
                Out of my mind.

I still remember
when I could not sleep
at three a.m.
And yet, today,
I find us new with laughter
here in the sun.
                Here in the sun.

For You From Sascha

SUMMERWIND

The one who owns this summer is not here,
not here to know the tender summerwind,
not here to share the glowing and the song.
The one who owns this summer did not live,
not live to touch the richness of this day,
this day in summer when you are alone.
Weep to the summerwind, weep and love again
the one you remember.

Days And Seasons

SUNRISE

Can it be true:
        this is an easy morning?
The day escaping from
        its dark confinements,
while sun starts brushing
        earth with silken warmth.
No strain at all.
No hurry anywhere.

Can it be true:
your mind is whole and steady.
Now you remember things
        as once they were
on other mornings, then,
        and other days...

Can it be true:
this is an easy morning?
Remembering does not hurt?
        And you can close your eyes,
        and you can see,
        can smile, at sunrise.

        This is an easy morning.
            Use it well.

For You From Sascha

NOW AUTUMN

What a strange time is autumn.
More than a season,
autumn can be like a mood.
Softness and warmth and abundance
drift from the sky like a smile.

And you remember the seasons
before the children died.

They do seem far away sometimes,
those seasons, now.
But not the children –
they are always here
in this strange time, this autumn,
when the softness
and the warmth
and the abundance
of unseen children
drift from the sky like a smile.

Days And Seasons

SEPTEMBER : MONARCHS

Time between summer and winter.
Time under changing skies –
muted and heavy with foresight,
or endless blue, smiling at butterflies.

Time between summer and winter.
Time between laughter and tear –
harvest of beauty remembered
and voices (where are you?) to hear.

Time between summer and winter,
thoughtful and painful and wise –
muted and heavy with losing,
but smiling at butterflies.

For You From Sascha

INDIAN SUMMER

This may well be
the softest time of all.
Does mild September
still surprise your mind
with memories you thought
you would not have?

Believe me, friend, that
(after many tears)
this may well be
the softest time of all.

Days And Seasons

NINO
born on October 28, 1953

Small son, you died
too many years ago.
You are so far away,
far in the past.

I have not spoken
to your photograph
how many years now?
I forgot to count...

I never dared imagine
(when you died)
the mindless water
burying your face.

But I remember still
the love between us.
And in remembering
I recognize:
your golden life
forever touches mine.

For You From Sascha

HALLOWEEN

It is here, this day of merriment
and children's pleasure.
Gremlins and goblins
and ghosties at the door
of your house.

And the other children
come to the door of your mind.
Faces out of the past,
small ghosts with sweet, painted faces.
They do not shout.

Those children
who no longer march laughing
on cold Halloween night,
they stand at the door of your mind –
and you will let them in,
so that you can give them
the small gifts of your Halloween –
        a smile and a tear.

Days And Seasons

NOVEMBER AGAIN

November again, almost winter.
Muted world outside,
faded red, misty yellow –
fog in the morning.
Even the hardest wind
seems kind enough,
because we know,
we know that stormy blades
lie waiting.

November again, almost winter.
Gently the heart reaches
for the awareness of things to
                            come.

Holidays, so we call them.
Gently, the heart turns to
                         Christmas -

Songs everywhere. And lights.
Gently the heart must remember
the things gone by,
the time gone by,
the child gone by.

November again.

For You From Sascha

To My Daughter Eve
born on November 4, 1950

How would it be if you were with me now?
What would we say, what would we do together?
I think we might be waiting for the frost,
and we would relish this October weather.

And would we worry over waistlines spreading?
Oh, surely we would speak about some beau.
But we would soon leave smallish talk behind us
to wonder over things we do not know.

And we would fret about the same old questions,
why do we make mistakes (and more than once)?
Why doesn't love stay new and strong and tender?
And why do people fill the world with guns?

I think we might be waiting for the frost,
and we would relish this Octoberweather.

What would we say, what would we do together?
How would it be if you were with me now?

Days And Seasons

IN FALL

Things often are
most beautiful
before they leave us -

As autumn ends,
she spends her final glory
on us, who hurt
when we remember spring.

For You From Sascha

HOW SOON ——

(How Soon Is Winter!)
Seasons racing by
with timeless haste –
      Spring just a fleeting moment
      — summer gone.

Then autumn holds the heart
with brief perfection.

How soon is winter.
And how much remembered
          underneath the snow
are songs, and flowers,
      harvest wealth
      and children.

Days And Seasons

GIVING THANKS

I can not hold your hands today;
I can not see your smile.
I can not hear your voices now,
My children, who are gone.

But I recall your faces well,
The songs, the talks, the sighs,
And storytimes, and winterwalks,
And sharing secret things.

I know you helped my mind to live
Beyond your time with me.
You gave me clearer eyes to see —
You gave me finer ears to hear —
What living means, what dying means,
My children, who are gone.

So here it is Thanksgiving Day,
And you are not with me.
And while I weep a mother's tear,
I thank you for the gift you were,
And all the gifts you gave to me,
My children, who are gone.

For You From Sascha

SPEAKING LOVE

Thoughtful mornings in November;
wintergray and chill at twilight.
Soon there will be colored candles.
Soon there will be celebration.

Do not force your heart from sorrow
at this time of happy splendor:
this is also time for speaking
love to dead and silent children.

Days And Seasons

WINTERSONG

Season of lights, season of love and peace,
Season of shadow, season of memories,
Season of warmth and joy, season of secret tears:

Give us the courage to laugh again.
Give us the vision to hope again.
Give us the power to love again —
                 For all our new seasons
                 And all our new years

For You From Sascha

HANUKKAH

When the time comes
for lighting festive candles,
let them remind you
not only of what you lost,
but also of what you had.

Days And Seasons

SOLSTICE

The year has turned again.
As quickly as it came,
it runs away.

The year has turned. Again
before us waits
another string
of sparkling celebrations ...

> How fine and welcome
>   are the holidays.
> How sharp and painful
>   are the holidays.

Dark with the light,
grief with the joy,
life tumbles on.

For You From Sascha

YULE

The song of yuletide rings
with tears and laughter.
    And if you listen deeply,
    you will find
    the sound of every voice
    you ever knew.

Days And Seasons

AT CHRISTMAS

I reach for the laughter of Christmas,
around me are music and light.
The air arches clear into heaven,
a mirror of gold and of white.

I touch it, the laughter of Christmas.
The stars are as near as my eyes.
I find in the laughter of Christmas
        your voice,
and too many good-byes.

For You From Sascha

LISTEN

A new year does arrive again at midnight.
Your mind is heavy with remembering.
Your heart must ache before another chance
to quarrel with the emptiness of time.

Yes, New Year does walk in again at midnight.
And can you hear it speak of comfort waiting,
of open doors and brighter rooms to enter —
of deeper meaning and of greater hope?

The new year will arrive and begs you:
                              LISTEN

Days And Seasons

LET THERE BE LIGHT?

The new year comes
when all the world is ready
for changes, resolutions –
great beginnings.

For us, to whom
that stroke of midnight means
a missing child remembered,
for us the new year comes
more like another darkness.

> But let us not forget
> that this may be the year
> when love and hope and courage
> find each other somewhere
> in the darkness
> > to lift their voice and speak:
> > let there be light.

For You From Sascha

'TIS THE SEASON

It is trying to be
A warm and a loving time,
With kindness and light,
And a feeling of hopeful renewal.

Find what blessings you can.
Help your heart to remember
That the children who died
Are about us, everywhere,
Trying to make this,
Even for you,
A warm and a loving time.

HOLIDAY FEELINGS

It is fitting that in this time of heightened emotional awareness, the memories about dead children assume a bittersweet priority. As our feelings of loss and pain mingle with the celebrations, memories are at once the burden and the blessing of this festive season, a cause for loving tears and a cause for aching smiles. Holiday feelings are intricate.

Let it be.

For You From Sascha

HEAR THE CHILDREN

We whose children died before us,
Do we share a greater wisdom?
True, beyond all earthly symbols?
Do we heed the heart's instruction?
Do we hear the children's voices?

Christmas is but one reminder
Of the legacy they left us.
Our dead, remembered children
Sing the same eternal song,
Send the same eternal message:

Peace is the question,
Love is the answer.

> David star or haunted cross,
> Crescent moon or sacred drum,
> Holy stream, ancestral shrine,
> Hymn or chant or temple dancer,
> All of us in Grieving Country,
> All of us share grievers' wisdom:

Peace is the question,
Love is the answer

Days And Seasons

AT NEW YEAR'S, TIME

Time does not touch
    the firmament of stars
with a simplicity
    of days and nights and years.
The rhythm of this smallness
    we call earth
is only whisper among galaxies.

Beyond the measured years
    which rise and fall,
beyond the calendars
    of human time and place,
the meaning of this smallness
    we call life
will find us somewhere
    in eternity.

CHANGES

Be aware that new grief
changes all of your emotions
for a time.

But grief does not change
all of your emotions
forever!

Some of your old feelings
will return to you.

Please be patient.

V. THE ROAD AHEAD

For You From Sascha

THAT ONE CHILD

We travel through this life
in many climates
(the weather calm sometimes,
but often fierce).
We find the sunshine
and endure the shadows.
We falter often on the road, at night.

And many walk with us
who claim no sorrow,
and some who meet us
say they have not cried.
The world, they say,
prefers its play and laughter.
They say, we are
      uncomfortable company.

Let them be what they seem
and keep from envy.
Remember only this:
They never were
as close as you have been
to that one child.

The Road Ahead

THEN AND NOW

They were my children, then.
Resounding voices, arguments and laughter –
Intense and wide awake at storytime –
In love with music, dance and birthday parties –

So serious about their great inventions –
So filled with promise, all-involved with life.

They are my children, now.
Remembered like a touching of the wind –
Remembered in the clarity of mornings –
Remembered in the smiles of other children –

Remembered like the charm of cradlesongs –
Alive in silence and in absence, present.
My children, now.

For You From Sascha

SUICIDE

Once you were rich with life.
You were self-confident
and filled with beauty,

until a darkness came
to seize your mind,
a force from out of silence,
an ache without a reason,
a pain without a name.

What was this darkness that
would not be conquered?
What force,
what reason,
what pain without a name
would use your hands to take
your life away.

Once you were rich with life;
you were self-confident
and filled with beauty.
Now we are left alone
without an answer.

PERMISSION TO GRIEVE

Give yourself permission to hurt and ask others to understand. It will be much better for all of you, if you keep from being too brave, too polite. That makes others feel more helpless, more distant from you, perhaps even a bit rejected.

If you can, talk very briefly to your immediate family, especially to your partner, and ask for patience, promising yours in return. Because we all react differently to great emotional strain, this can be a time of temporary estrangements in your family -This is also the time to remember all the reasons why you loved each other in the first place. Don't worry about feeling 'nothing': your mind has been dealt a terrible blow, and your old feelings will need time to return.

Do let others give you evidence of their devotion, concern, warmth, attention, empathy - after all, these are the finest gifts we can give to each other. And believe me: honesty in sharing your feelings is a gift from you to them, showing your friends and your helpers that you trust them, that they are important and that they are appreciated.

For You From Sascha

LAUGHTER

Grief is such a serious thing. It breaks your life apart, it leaves you confused and powerless.

Grief is a pain beyond words; grief is relentless force; grief will not yield the field without an enormous struggle. And yet, in the middle of all this emotional hardship there waits a deep and resonant intuition saying 'LIFE GOES ON' - and does it also say 'YOU WILL HEAL?' Is there something in our spirit that keeps us breathing, waiting for the daylight, ready (even against our will) to live again?

Surely, tears ARE unavoidable - but what about laughter? Does it seem that both tears AND laughter will help us to keep going, to live again, and to enjoy life again some day? And can we come to see laughter as an affirmation of our dead children? We would not want to tell them, would we, that their life is the cause of our unremitting sadness from this day forward?

Make your life ready for laughter.

COMPASSION

Compassion is such an easy word, yet it is not at all easy to achieve. Compassion means suspending one's own critical and advisory inclinations to help someone. Compassion is leaving oneself outside. Compassion is not approval.

What the other person may need is often not at all what the compassionate helper believes to be helpful. The helper may want to give advice, or talk about himself/herself. What the griever needs, however, may well be a listener, a focused attention on the griever and on the loss the griever sustained.

Often, compassion means not doing something - listening rather than speaking, crying rather than comforting with words.

Compassion is not an easy task, but it is among the greatest gifts we can give to each other.

For You From Sascha

STARTING SMALL

Forgiveness is especially important
at times of grieving.

Forgiveness is especially important
for the griever.

Forgiveness must not be forced.

Begin with small easy things.
First forgive what
you can forgive without straining.
Then try forgiving some deeper
disappointments - one at a time.

The Road Ahead

VARIATIONS

Alone
    on winternights
    when darkness stands
    within your house,
    a sullen guest.

Alone
    at summernoon
    when beauty seems
    to be an empty space
    between the thing you see
    and what you feel...

Alone
    when some old song
    reverses time and place
    and you remember
    something that was best.
    And you are suddenly
    alive with love -
    and nothing else,
    not even sorrow
    breaks the glow

Alone?

SURVIVAL

When my grief was new, my pain felt interminable. My mind had no power to help me, because I was filled with or surrounded by the most desperate, confused feelings - which I know now are the nature of grief and are an appropriate reaction to great loss. I surrendered to grief, when I sensed that I did not have the mental and physical ammunition for fighting the battle against what seemed to be this ultimate enemy.

The extremes of my grief, by coincidence, served to enforce two insights: I HURT and I was ALIVE. Very gradually I began to realize that in the process of healing, even small successes are rewarding. And since I did not have any big successes, I climbed back into life on a ladder of small successes.

How about YOU?

The Road Ahead

TEACHER AND HELPER

This is a time
When you do not listen
To yourself.
This is the time
When you do not want
To recognize your needs.
Taking care of yourself
Is such a meaningless notion now.

Yet, these days
More than any others,
Must have your help
In guarding your survival.

Life asks that you go on
     In your child's honor,
Because you will be a teacher.
Because you will be a helper.
Because you will be the keeper
     Of your child's memory.

For You From Sascha

WISH

I wish you gentle days
and quiet nights.
I wish you memories
to keep you strong.

I wish you time to smile
and time for song.

And then I wish you friends
to give you love,
when you are hurt and lost
and life is blind.

I wish you friends and love
and peace of mind.

The Road Ahead

HUMOR

Is there a place for humor in a griever's life? Could humor be a bridge between pain and hope? Our sense of humor will probably have a hard time getting restarted, and that's natural. At first, laughter may serve only as a reminder of our lost ability to enjoy life - but finally, laughter may become a promise for hope and healing

Of course, we must be careful not to rush ourselves or other grievers into humor, but we can give laughter a place in our grieving. Laughter is not disrespectful to the dead. The humor we can welcome into our grieving lives helps us to do the best we can, for ourselves and for the memory of the children who are lost to us.

For You From Sascha

PERENNIALS

Good memories

are the perennials

that bloom again

after the hard winter of grief—

begins to yield to hope.

The Road Ahead

EPILOGUE

Beyond the history of grand events,
behind the memory of battles fought,
of freedoms lost and won,
there stand the silent legends of this earth,
the monuments of human joy and sorrow.
a sky of laughter on a sea of tears.

And they who cried the tears,
their children fallen,
sisters, brothers dead -
with lives washed over by relentless grief
they fought the battles seldom writ in stone.

And they who cried the tears
and laughed the laughter—
(though we may not be told
their name and place),
they share with us the history of coping,
of courage tested and enduring hope.

And they who cried the tears
and laughed the laughter
are history, as much as swords at war,
as much as grand events and freedoms won.

continued

For You From Sascha

And all who ever mourned
-the whole world over -
are quietly with you and me today
to walk with us
through grief to hope and healing.

> Written for the 13th Annual Conference of
> The Compassionate Friends
> on July 6-8, 1990 in Philadelphia

The Road Ahead

WHEN GRIEVING FRIENDS MEET

We are here together
in the radiance of our memories
and in the darkness of our loss

The memories of days gone by
can be like northern lights,
outshining distance and night,
rising in wonder.

And sometimes
the radiance of our memories overcomes
the darkness of our loss.

We are here together
in the radiance of our memories
and in the service of our love.

Dedicated to the International Conference
NORTHERN LIGHTS OF HEALING
Les Amis Compatissants du Canada/
The Compassionate Friends
2000 A. D.

For You From Sascha

REMINDER

We who were left behind
to know the shadows -
We who were left behind
to touch the night -
We who were left behind
to heal the darkness
and to share this day -

    We who have turned once more
    to hope and loving,
    though we were given graves
    and lifeless children:
        We hear them now,
        these children and their song
        reminding us,
        reminding us again,
        that we must fill the time
        we spend in life
        with understanding,
        tenderness and peace.

The Road Ahead

TO THE DEAD INFANTS

They are gone
these young hearts
these flawless souls.
They are gone
and we must grieve
their loss –
we must remember.

But when we
begin to live again,
then we can be
each one of us
a heritage of humanness
a memorial of hope
a sign of closer understanding.
    In their name
    who are gone,
    these young hearts
    these flawless souls –
    in their name
    let our lives
        grow

(The Compassionate Friends in Brandon, Manitoba, Canada, chose the last lines of this text for their Childrens' Memorial, which this author had the honor to dedicate in May 1991).

For You From Sascha

SMILES

The smiles of our children fill this room
With memories of other summer days
When we could hear their laughter in the morning
When they could share the songs we sang at night.

The smiles of our children find us here
With all the loving that we gave them once
To bring us courage for another morning
To comfort us when we feel hurt at night.

The smiles of our children touch us now
With quiet hands of comfort and of hope.
Let them remind us as we meet today
That we are friends in our children's names.

Let us remember as we meet today
What our children taught us with their lives:
That love is never lost and love is never in vain.

Written for the Second National IN LOVING MEMORY Conference Reston, Virginia 1997

IN LOVING MEMORY
May 1999
For the Fourth Conference in Vienna, Virginia

In spirit alike and with homage enduring, we came
Honoring love and remembrance in our child's name

Closely together in tender communion we stand
Holding each other's heart in a tremulous hand.
Children surround us that nobody's eye can see,
Children whose blessings bring solace to you and me.

Starting alone in the memory of heartbreaking fears,
Let us now share our sorrow and ease our tears.

In loving devotion let hope and fine courage arise,
Bestowed in the spirit of children beyond our eyes.
Until, in spite of the hurt from unbearable loss, we find
The treasure of friendship here and new peace of mind.

ABOUT THE AUTHOR

Sascha was born in Bremen, Germany (of Bremen Town musicians' fame). She emigrated to the United States in 1947 and studied literature and history at the Universities of Colorado (B.A.) and Denver (M.A.).

Sascha's daughter Eve was born in November 1950; her son Nino arrived in October 1953. Nino drowned three and a half years later, and on the 15th anniversary of his death, Eve died of suicide.

After spending some thirty years in various areas of mental health work, Sascha initiated a professional support service for persons with panic disorders and/or agoraphobia. For the last 16 years, she has been providing bereavement care and grief support, often by telephone. She has provided workshops in Germany, in Canada, and at IN LOVING MEMORY conferences, as well as speaking to Compassionate Friends groups and conference audiences. In 1998, Sascha was honored with the award for TCF Professional of the Year.

After several years as editor of The Compassionate Friends' Central Iowa Chapter, Sascha started the quarterly publication of L.A.R.G.O. (Life After Repeated Grief: Options) which has a farflung readership in the USA, Canada, Germany, South Africa and Australia.

About the Author

Other than three smaller volumes of writing, Sascha has published "The Sorrow And The Light" (1992) and "Wintersun" (1996).

Sascha now lives in retirement near Denver, Colorado under the careful supervision of the feline pundits Puczicam and Susie Q. (and an occasional stray), who help to find all the papers, keys, glasses, hearing aids and garage door openers Sascha regularly misplaces.

Made in the USA
Lexington, KY
16 November 2011